# Birds of Prey



Johanna Rohan

## Contents

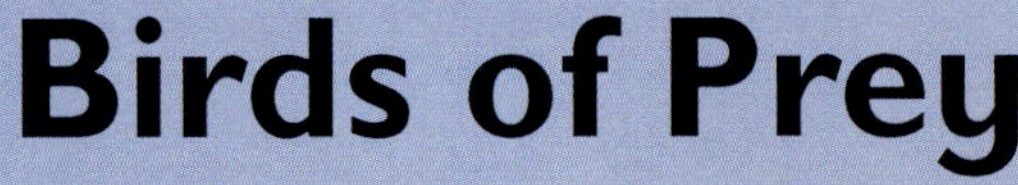

# Birds of Prey

Some of the world's best **predators** don't have teeth and claws. They have beaks and **talons**. These are the birds of prey.

**Raptor**

Birds of prey are also known as raptors.

Birds of prey are strong hunters. They catch and kill other animals to eat.

a Bald Eagle

**Small Males**

Mostly, female birds of prey are much larger than males.

There are around 300 **species** of birds of prey in the world. They can be sorted into groups.

These groups are:

kites
falcons
owls
hawks

Birds of prey have excellent eyesight, smell and hearing. These **senses** help them to search for and hunt their prey.

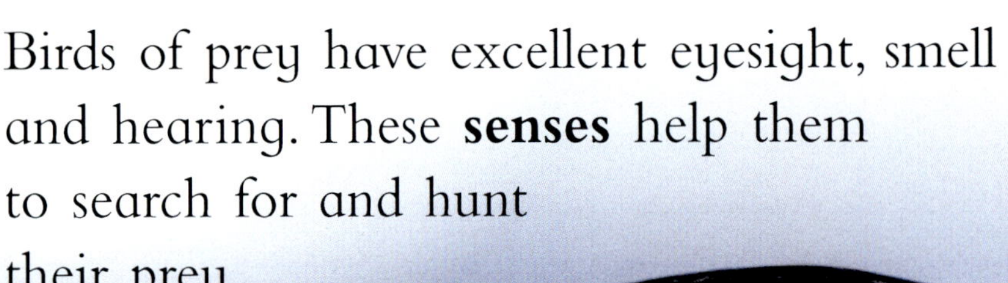

**Eye Spy**

A Bald Eagle's eyesight is so good it can see a fish while flying hundreds of metres above the water.

**Eagle Eyes**

If we could see as well as an eagle, we could stand 250 bus lengths away from a rabbit and see it twitch its ears!

The Turkey Vulture has one of the best senses of smell of all the birds of prey. It can smell and find food even while flying high in the air.

Some owls, such as the Barn Owl, can find their prey in darkness. They do this by using their amazing sense of hearing.

Birds of prey have strong, powerful feet with curved, sharp talons. This helps them to catch, hold and kill their prey.



**Sharp Talons**

A falcon's back talons are so sharp they would be able to cut through your wrist!

Birds of prey have special beaks. Their beaks are very sharp and are shaped like hooks. This helps them to stab and rip meat.

**Good Eaters**

Birds of prey rip meat into small pieces to swallow.

**Clever Feet**

Birds of prey use their feet, not their beaks, to catch their prey.

# The Eagles

Eagles are very powerful birds of prey. Most eagles are larger than any other raptors, except the vultures. Eagles have large beaks, huge feet and talons, and big **wingspans**.

### Up High

Eagles build their nests in tall trees or on high cliffs.

### Eagles

| | |
|---|---|
| **Size:** | very large birds of prey |
| **Diet:** | fish, lizards, snakes, other birds, and even monkeys, pigs and goats! |
| **Lifespan:** | around 30 years in the wild |

*a Golden Eagle*

## The Wedge-tailed Eagle

Many eagles are found in Europe, Asia and Africa. But one of the world's largest eagles can be found in Australia – the Wedge-tailed Eagle. These eagles have wedge-shaped tails, and wingspans of 2.5 metres.

### Dinner Time

Wedge-tailed Eagles have been known to form a team to hunt large animals like kangaroos and wallabies.

*a Wedge-tailed Eagle*

# The Hawks

Hawks live mostly in forest areas. Long tails and short, rounded wings help hawks fly quickly and steer sharply. Most hawks hunt their prey by dashing from a hiding spot.

### Types of Hawks

Harriers and Buzzards are types of hawks.

*a Harrier*

*a Buzzard*

### Hunting

The Goshawk mostly hunts small mammals and birds.

### Hawks

| | |
|---|---|
| **Size:** | medium-sized birds of prey |
| **Diet:** | small mammals, reptiles, insects and sometimes other birds |
| **Lifespan:** | around 25 years in the wild |

## The Goshawk

The Goshawk lives in forest areas in the Northern Hemisphere. It has short, broad wings with a wingspan of 1.2 metres. Its long tail helps it fly swiftly through the forest.

A leather strap is used in falconry to hold the bird.

### Falconry Birds

Goshawks are used as **falconry birds** because of their speed and bravery.

A leather glove protects the falconer's hand.

# The Falcons

Falcons have long, pointed wings to help them fly at high speed and change direction quickly. Narrow, bumpy toes help them grip their prey.

**Take Over!**

Falcons don't build their own nests. Instead, they take over old nests of other birds. Sometimes, they lay eggs in tree hollows.

**Falcons**

| | |
|---|---|
| **Size:** | small-to-medium-sized birds of prey |
| **Diet:** | smaller birds, reptiles and small land animals |
| **Lifespan:** | around 17 years in the wild |

## The Peregrine Falcon

The Peregrine Falcon is the fastest animal on Earth. Its speed helps it catch its prey, which is mostly other birds. It hits its prey at high speed in the air. This kills the prey.

### High-speed Flyer

The Peregrine Falcon has been recorded flying at speeds of over 400 km per hour. That's as fast as the fastest train on Earth!

# The Ospreys

Ospreys are large birds with wingspans of 1.8 metres. They are found all over the world near lakes, rivers and seas. They have long, narrow wings and short tails.

The Osprey is sometimes called the Sea Hawk.

**Ospreys**

| | |
|---|---|
| **Size:** | large birds of prey |
| **Diet:** | fish |
| **Lifespan:** | around 30 years in the wild |

## Catching Prey

The Osprey flies slowly over water, looking for its prey. When it sees a fish, it **hovers**. Then it dives feet first into the water to grab it. It can close its nostrils and dive up to one metre underwater!

**Good Grip**

Ospreys have rough pads on their feet. This helps them to grab and hold onto slippery fish!

# The Kites

Kites have long wings, short legs and weak feet. They are found in warm areas around the world. Kites glide and **soar** through the air. They quickly **swoop** to catch their prey.

**Kind Hunters**

Unlike other birds of prey, kites are not **aggressive** hunters.

## The Black-shouldered Kite

The Black-shouldered Kite is a small, pale-grey raptor found in Australia. Black-shouldered Kites mostly eat mice. But they will also eat grasshoppers, rats and even rabbits.

### Kites

| | |
|---|---|
| **Size:** | small, light birds of prey |
| **Diet:** | insects, small animals and even dead animals |
| **Lifespan:** | around 20 years in the wild |

### Shoulder Patches

The Black-shouldered Kite has a black edge to its wing. When it sits, it looks like it has black shoulders.

Black-shouldered Kites have wingspans of just under one metre.

# The Owls

Owls are **nocturnal** birds of prey found around the world. They have flat faces, small hooked beaks and large eyes that face forwards. Owls have short tails and rounded wings. Most owls only hunt at night.

**Down in One!**

Most owls swallow their prey whole. Then they spit out any fur, feathers or bones.

## Owls

| | |
|---|---|
| **Size:** | small-to-medium-sized birds of prey |
| **Diet:** | small animals, insects, other birds and fish |
| **Lifespan:** | around 60 years in the wild |

*an African Great Horned Owl*

## The Snowy Owl

The Snowy Owl is found in the Arctic. It is a large owl with yellow eyes, a black beak and a wingspan of 1.5 metres. It keeps warm by having thick feathers, as well as feathers on its feet and toes.

Snowy Owls get their name because they are almost pure white. The Snowy Owl mainly eats **lemmings** and **voles**.

**Hunting All Hours**

It does not get dark in the Arctic summer so Snowy Owls can hunt in the day or night.

# The Vultures

Vultures have long, broad wings. This helps them soar long distances for food. Vultures are **scavengers**. They do not often kill their own prey.

| **Vultures** | |
|---|---|
| **Size:** | very large birds of prey |
| **Diet:** | dead or dying animals |
| **Lifespan:** | most vultures live for around 30 years in the wild, although some can live for much longer |

*a Griffon Vulture*

## The Andean Condor

The Andean Condor is a vulture. It's one of the largest flying birds in the world. It has a wingspan of over 3 metres! It is black with white feathers around its neck. It lives in the Andes mountain range in South America.

Andean Condors eat large dead animals, such as deer or cattle.

### Ripe Old Age

The Andean Condor can live up to 60 years in the wild.

### Bald Head

Vultures have bald heads. If vultures had head feathers, they would get spattered with blood when they ate dead animals. This would be very hard to clean!

# Endangered Birds of Prey

About 25 types of birds of prey around the world are **endangered**.

These birds are endangered because of:

- **habitat loss**
- **poaching**
- **pollution**.

The Californian Condor is a very endangered species.

Habitat loss has meant some birds of prey have lost their homes.

Some endangered birds of prey around the world are:

Crowned Eagle

Philippine Eagle

Philippine Eagle
Egyptian Vulture
Crowned Eagle
Indian White-rumped Vulture

Egyptian Vulture

Indian White-rumped Vulture

**CASE STUDY**

## The Californian Condor

The Californian Condor is close to **extinction**. Over the years, people have shot or poisoned many of them.

The Californian Condor has a huge wingspan of around 3 metres.

### Is It a Bird? Is It a Plane?

Californian Condors have been mistaken for small aeroplanes because they are so big when they soar!

### Californian Condor

| | |
|---|---|
| **Size:** | one of the largest birds of prey |
| **Diet:** | dead animals, such as cattle and deer |
| **Habitat:** | rocky scrubland, forests and savannas |
| **Lifespan:** | around 50 years |

In 1990, there were no Californian Condors left in the wild. People wanted to help, so Californian Condors were **bred** in zoos and wildlife parks. Over time, some birds have been set free, back into the wild.

Today, there are 327 Californian Condors left in the world.

**Caring for Chicks**

This chick was bred in a zoo. A puppet that looks like an adult condor is used to care for it. The chick thinks the puppet is its mother!

# Saving Birds of Prey

There are many ways to help save endangered birds of prey.

1. Birds are being bred in zoos and wildlife parks.
2. People are making sure that the wild places where birds of prey live are looked after.
3. Zoos and wildlife parks are teaching people about birds of prey.

**A Helping Hand**
A vet is helping this condor chick to hatch at a zoo.

This falconer is teaching school children about birds of prey.

## Easy Pickings

In Africa many 'vulture restaurants' have been set up. These restaurants are a safe place for vultures to find food. People donate dead animals such as cows and zebras for the vultures to eat.

This African White-backed Vulture is feeding on a dead zebra at a vulture restaurant in Namibia, Africa.

# It's Quiz Time!

Here are five questions to test your bird of prey knowledge. The answers are on page 32 – good luck!

**Question 1**
What is another name for a bird of prey?

**Question 2**
True or false? Male birds of prey are usually larger than the females.

**Question 3**
What type of bird of prey is used as a falconry bird?

**Question 4**
What is the fastest animal on Earth?

**Question 5**
True or false? The Andean Condor is a type of vulture.

*a Northern Goshawk*

# Glossary

an Indian White-rumped Vulture

**aggressive**
strong and active

**bred**
born in captivity

**endangered**
when an animal species is in danger of extinction

**extinction**
when a species of plant or animal dies out forever

**falconry birds**
birds of prey trained for the sport of falconry

**habitat loss**
the loss of an animal's home

**hovers**
floats in the air

**lemmings**
small animals that are like rats

**nocturnal**
active at night

**poaching**
killing an animal that is endangered

**pollution**
things that harm the environment

**predators**
animals that hunt and kill other animals

**scavengers**
animals that feed on dead animals

**senses**
an animal's sight, hearing and smell

**soar**
to fly high in the air

**species**
a group of animals that are alike

**swoop**
to fly down upon something

**talons**
the claws of birds of prey

**voles**
small animals like mice

**wingspans**
the lengths of birds' wings, from tip to tip

# Index

**Quiz Answers**
Question 1: raptor
Question 2: false
Question 3: Goshawk
Question 4: Peregrine Falcon
Question 5: true